GW00983863

Truth and Unity in Christian Fellowship

2ND APRIL 2007

HOSTED BY THE PETERBOROUGH DIOCESAN EVANGELICAL
FELLOWSHIP IN PARTNERSHIP WITH THE LATIMER TRUST

AT CHRIST THE KING, KETTERING

BY THE RT REVD DR MICHAEL NAZIR-ALI

BISHOP OF ROCHESTER

The Latimer Trust

© Michael Nazir-Ali 2007

ISBN 978-0-946307-92-0

Published by the Latimer Trust

PO Box 26685

London N14 4XQ

www.latimertrust.org

CONTENTS

1 John 1:1-10 (RSV)

That which was from the beginning, which we have heard, which we have seen with our eyes, which we have looked upon and touched with our hands, concerning the word of life – the life was made manifest, and we saw it, and testify to it, and proclaim to you the eternal life which was with the Father and was made manifest to us – that which we have seen and heard we proclaim also to you, so that you may have fellowship with us; and our fellowship is with the Father and with his Son Jesus Christ. And we are writing this that our joy may be complete.

This is the message we have heard from him and proclaim to you, that God is light and in him is no darkness at all. If we say we have fellowship with him while we walk in darkness, we lie and do not live according to the truth; but if we walk in the light, as he is in the light, we have fellowship with one another, and the blood of Jesus his Son cleanses us from all sin. If we say we have no sin, we deceive ourselves, and the truth is not in us. If we confess our sins, he is faithful and just, and will forgive our sins and cleanse us from all unrighteousness. If we say we have not sinned, we make him a liar, and his word is not in us.

1.   A basis for Fellowship and a basis for Unity

This is a very important passage about the topic of truth and unity in Christian fellowship. It is about unity in the fellowship, but it is also about the basis for that fellowship and the basis for that unity. I return to it again and again because it is such a positive chapter, and yet it addresses very directly some of the problems that we have been encountering in the last few years.

The first thing about this chapter is the apostolic witness. It is the testimony of those who were with Jesus, who heard him, saw him, felt him, touched him, knew him. They say that this experience of Jesus has led them to fellowship with the Father who sent Him. They then express the desire that this ·experience of Jesus, and this revelation of the Father to them in Jesus, should also be the basis of the fellowship of all Christians with the apostolic band. Then they say that we cannot claim to be in fellowship with the Father and the Son, and with the band of the apostles who are in fellowship with the Father and the Son, if we live in ways that deny the basis of this fellowship.

They are not claiming that there is a perfect church. They are quite clear about the reality of sin, even in the justified believer and even in God's holy people, and they set out the way for that sin to be dealt with.

2.   Apostolic Testimony

First, let us consider the apostolic testimony. There is a very real sense in which we can say that the church is made by the apostolic teaching. The apostolic teaching is received, it is lived, and it is passed on from generation to generation, from person to person, across different cultures and throughout the world. What is the apostolic teaching? It is the story of God's saving work among his people and in his world. God's saving purposes have been revealed once for all in Jesus Christ in a way that is unique.

When we think about Jesus, what are we saying about him, about his person and work in terms of the apostolic preaching? We are saying something about what Jesus taught about ourselves, about God, about God's world. We are saying something about who he thought he was. This is important today, because often people give a lot of attention to what Jesus is supposed to have said, but not enough to what he said he was – his own self-understanding. In this connection there are four things that are worth noting.

2.1. Jesus as God's wisdom

The first is the increasing realisation among New Testament scholars that Jesus thought of himself as God's wisdom, that wisdom who had brought the world into being, that wisdom of God who has been with God from the very beginning. Remember the incident where John sends his disciples to Jesus, to ask Jesus whether he is the one who is to come or should they look for another (Matt. 11:2-15). Jesus replies to them in terms of Isaiah 35, a passage about God. He then turns to the other listeners and says, 'Wisdom is justified by her actions' (v. 19). Later in the chapter, he refers to his yoke that he wants us to take on ourselves (v. 29). This refers directly back to passages in the apocrypha about the yoke of wisdom, which makes us wise. The queen of the South, he says, came to hear Solomon and his wisdom and then he goes on to say that someone greater than Solomon is here (Matt. 12:42). And there are many passages in the first three gospels and elsewhere which show how Jesus understood himself as the wisdom of God present to his people.

2.2. Jesus as the Son of Man

We have got a young scholar in our diocese, Andy Angel, who has been doing some very interesting linguistic work on the use of the term the 'son of man', examining how it might have been used in the Aramaic of Jesus' time, and how it came to be expressed in the Greek. From this he has begun to show that Jesus' use of the term is not simply self-referential. It is not just a general term about human beings, but in some contexts at least, it refers to the heavenly figure who receives divine honours. I have also noticed that in Daniel 7, when the heavenly figure comes to the Ancient of Days, it says all nations will serve him (Dan. 7:14). This word, translated 'serve', is only ever used for God. This is just a small point but I think it is significant.

2.3. Jesus as Divine Messiah

Thirdly, Jesus understood himself as Messiah. Obviously he was reluctant to acknowledge the Messiah-ship that people wanted him to, and there were good reasons for that. Tom Wright has pointed out again and again that the understanding of Messiah at the time of Jesus was of a human figure, and that appears to be the case. However, if you consider the Bible as a whole, then the figure of the Messiah also appears strongly in a divine light. For example, Psalm 2:7 ('You are my son this day I have begotten you'), and Psalm 45:6 ('Your throne, O God, is forever and ever'), are both said about the Messiah. Similarly, consider the testimony of Psalm 110:1, to which the NT refers so often: 'The LORD said to my Lord, sit at my right hand until I make your enemies a footstool for your feet.' Similarly, in the prophets, where God is spoken of as the Shepherd of Israel, the Messiah is immediately associated with him (e.g., Ezek. 34). Moreover, the way in which Jesus understood himself as Messiah has to be related to the other ways in which he thought of himself.

2.4. Jesus' Miracles

In this connection, what Jesus did also shows who he thought that he was. A good illustration of this comes from Raageh Omar's series some time ago on the Miracles of Jesus. When the BBC decided that a Muslim should present a series on the miracles of Jesus I was a little surprised, I have to confess. But, to be fair, it was a very suggestive series, and in some ways more believing than some other series we have seen about Jesus from the BBC. But what struck me most forcibly about that series was that the narrator came to the conclusion that the miracles of Jesus showed his divinity. For a Muslim to come to that conclusion was very illuminating, because of course Islam has a tradition about the miracles of Jesus, but also at the same time a denial that he is divine.

So, the apostolic teaching, based on Jesus' own self-understanding is about who Jesus thought he was. But it is also about what Jesus did.

3.   What Jesus did

Here, we need to maintain an objective view of the atonement. Of course Jesus' suffering on the cross is an example to us. Of course we must take up our crosses and follow him. But it is much more than that. Jesus' death was a transaction which creates something new, which makes it possible for us to be who we are and where we are. Jesus stood in our place, and did what we are unable and unwilling to do. In this radical act of obedience, he turned away God's anger from us and from our rebellion and sinfulness. And so he is our substitute and representative. Of course he is also the great victor, but the atonement is not just about one thing. We have to keep these different ideas of the atonement together. So the apostolic preaching is about who Jesus is and what Jesus has done for us. It is also about the glorification of Jesus in his resurrection. This has great relevance not only to us in terms of our personal destiny; it also has to do with the renewal and transformation of creation. Indeed, as Oliver O'Donovan has insisted for so many years, our moral thinking about ourselves, about the church, about the world, is based not only on creation, but also on the resurrection.[1]

As we have seen, this apostolic testimony is taught down the ages and across cultures. However, sometimes the church neglects or forgets some aspect of that testimony. It is obscured by human sinfulness, by compromises that we make with the world around us. And so, from time to time, it is right that some aspect of this testimony is recovered and renewed in the church. An obvious example of this is the way in which the work of God's Holy Spirit in the life of believers and in the church has been powerfully recovered in the last century. Whatever we may think of what has happened on the extremes, that has been something that is of huge importance to the church today.

4.   The Bible as our norm

However, if the question arises whether something is part of the apostolic testimony, how is that matter settled? This is again an issue for us today. When we have to decide what it is that is apostolic in the church and for the church, then we have to refer to a norm. That norm is the Bible. The Bible enables us to decide what is authentically apostolic and what is not. This is, of course, one of the reasons why the Bible has been so central in the Anglican tradition. The Bible has been studied seriously in so many ways because of its importance. Some people try to suggest that the more you study the Bible the less important it becomes. That is not my experience, and it has not been the experience of those who have held to the centrality of the Scriptures in the Christian church, and certainly in the Anglican tradition. Of course, when we study the Bible we want to know how it was put

---

[1] See Oliver O'Donovan, *Resurrection and Moral Order: An Outline for Evangelical Ethics*, 2nd edition (Leicester: Apollos; Grand Rapids: Eerdmans, 1994).

together, what the literary traditions behind it are, what the oral traditions are, what were the interests of the authors: we do not in any way deny the human side of the Bible. Nevertheless, we affirm at the same time the providential side: that in all this human undertaking, God worked so that there might be an inspired and inspiring record of his purposes.

This is very different from how Muslims, for example, understand the Koran. There, any attempt at historical or literary research is blocked simply because the Koran is believed to be the word of God in a direct way, without human intervention of any kind. But that is not our view of the Bible, and the reason that people have studied different aspects of the Bible is precisely so that the Word of God, as it is revealed in the Bible, may become clearer, so that the Bible may function better as the norm by which the church lives.

5. The Bible in culture and context

However, we must also recognise that the Bible is used, and the apostolic testimony is given, in different situations, in different languages, in different cultures, and at different times. And so the question of how the Bible relates to culture and context becomes a lively one for us, and in our rapidly changing world it is very lively indeed. Anyone with a truly missionary heart will take cultural questions seriously. Those who translate the Bible into different languages know the seriousness of the problems that arise. How much of the spiritual culture of a people to take into account? What word to use for God? What word to use for the Spirit? What to say about the story of God's saving work in a particular culture, with its own background and its own history? Bible translators struggle with these questions all the time.[2] So, we must take

---

[2] Lamin Sanneh, *Translating the Message: The Missionary Impact on Culture*

6

seriously the question of how the apostolic message is communicated in different cultures, at different times, and in different places.

However, there are some boundaries to observe in the relationship of the apostolic message to culture or even to context,[3] of which two are worth mentioning. The first is the nature of the gospel itself. In the process of inculturation, of addressing the culture, nothing can be done that denies the very basis of the gospel. For instance, if a culture did not have a strong doctrine of creation, you could not translate the gospel into that culture without developing one. There are many cultures in the world that have no real doctrine of creation, cultures formed by Hinduism, or Buddhism for example. In such a culture, you could not say, 'In their world view there is no doctrine of creation, so let's forget about it!' If a culture is weak about personal human destiny, which many are, you could not say in the process of inculturation, 'This culture doesn't have a proper doctrine of personhood, so let's forget about that!' The process of inculturation must not in any way deny what is essential to the gospel itself.

Secondly, inculturation should not work against Christian fellowship. Returning to 1 John, Christian fellowship is based on certain things and nothing in inculturation should make that fellowship among Christians more difficult. When I go to South Africa, I should be able to discern the essentials of the gospel among the Christians in South Africa, and when they come here, the same should happen. We cannot, because of a process of inculturation, produce forms of the Christian faith that are entirely opaque to Christians elsewhere.

(Maryknoll: Orbis Books, 1989) tracks theological questions raised by Bible translators in the African context, and is hugely illuminating in this respect.
[3] By culture, I mean the customs, habits, language, and thought forms of the people; context has more to do with the socio-economic situation.

6.   The Gospel in culture and context

This is a very important issue in our present situation, because some people are claiming that their cultural situation requires them to express their Christian faith in a way that is very difficult for Christians in other parts of the world to understand. Therefore, for this process of the gospel's relationship to culture to flourish, we need certain criteria.   Bible translators, of course, have an immediate task, which is to render the Scriptures into a particular language.   But the Christian life, and the life of the Church, is about more than just the availability of the Scriptures.   So, what are the criteria?   You could say they have to do with intelligibility: the Christian faith as a whole has to become intelligible in terms of a particular culture or context.   However, although we must talk about intelligibility, we must talk about holiness at the same time. It is not just understanding the gospel but living the gospel that is important.   The apostolic teaching is given, received, and passed on in the context of the church.   It is not just isolated believers, or campaigning groups, who are trying to receive and pass on their testimony.   It has to do with the church itself.   But what do we mean when we speak of 'the church'?

In the New Testament we find there is first of all the church in people's homes.   Of course, those homes were not like our homes; they were extended households with extended families, servants, and slaves.   Nevertheless, one of the things that you can say about the New Testament household churches is that they were characterised by likeness: people were like one another.   We talk about family likeness.   You could say that about the church in people's homes.   These days, when we have so much talk about 'fresh expressions' (an expression that is becoming distinctly unfresh), you will find that they are churches that are characterised by likeness: people who like to do things in a particular way, or who live in a particular place, or have particular interests.   I used to think that this was not the right way to be church; I used to think that for church to be really church you must have unlikeness. However, I have revised that view, and now think that you can be

8

church which is characterised by likeness.

However, that is not the only manifestation of church, and it is not the only manifestation of church to which people should belong. There is also in the New Testament the church in the town or the city and, in fact, all our letters in the New Testament are addressed to such churches: Rome, Corinth, Ephesus, etc. This church is characterised by unlikeness – people of different social status, the young and the old, the slave and the free, women and men. That is why, for example, the instruction given about celebrating the Supper of our Lord in 1 Corinthians 11 presupposes a church of those who are unlike one another.

7. A universal Anglican tradition?

How does this likeness and unlikeness, this locality and universality, appear in Anglicanism?

7.1. Characteristic gatherings

After the Reformation, was the church of the household found anywhere? Perhaps it was found in family prayers. Actually, there is a very strong body of opinion that is trying to show that the advance of secularism is directly related to the decline of family religion. Callum Brown claims that it was not a decline, but a sudden demise.[4] Nevertheless, whatever you think about that, I think there is a relationship between the demise of family religion and the advance of secularisation.

The parish church is more like the church of the town or the city, the place where people who are unlike one another should

---

[4] Callum Brown, *The Death of Christian Britain: Understanding Secularisation, 1800-2000* (London; New York: Routledge, 2001).

be able to meet. However, the New Testament also has a strong sense of the church's universality, not simply because of the unlikeness of people in these city churches, but also because of the relationship of these churches to one another. Think, for example, of 2 Corinthians 8 and 9, and the desire to give aid to the church in Judea. Or think of the understanding of the church that we find in Ephesians and Colossians.

If we think of the church in these ways, certain things follow. What we have to agree is that at whatever level, whether it is in the home, the parish church, or the church universal, certain things need to be true of God's people. Their gifts have to be discerned; their Christian life has to be nurtured; they have to be enabled in the ministry to which God is calling them; those who have been given a particular responsibility to speak in Christ's name (which is what the Articles say about Christian ministers) should be enabled to do so. However, most significantly, the marks of the church are that it is one, holy, catholic, and apostolic. So, how does the church become that?

7.2.   Characteristic worship

First, the church becomes one, holy, catholic and apostolic through worship. That must be the church's primary calling, to worship God. Therefore, worship should have a primary call on our time as Christians, individually and corporately. The church becomes one, holy, catholic, and apostolic through the preaching of the Word and the celebration of the Sacraments. At the time of the Reformation it was said again and again, on every side, that the church is constituted by the preaching of the Word and the reverent and due administration of the Sacraments. Indeed, the celebration of the Sacraments is nothing other than the Word made visible.

7.3.   Characteristic behaviour

Secondly, though, the church is also made one holy, catholic, and apostolic, by holiness of life, and there is no way in which you can separate doctrine from morals. The absurd attempt in the last few years to say that there is something called 'core doctrine' and there is something called 'morals' is completely untenable. Our theology (what we believe about God) is closely tied up with anthropology (what we believe about men and women); the two cannot be separated. So holiness of life is involved in maintaining the church in its unity and its catholicity; it is not an optional extra.

This raises the question of discipline in the church. At the time of the Reformation, there was extensive argument about the place of discipline in the church: is it essential for the very being of the church, or is it just about good order? Many of the reformers were wary of the extensive discipline of the mediaeval church and did not want to replicate it. However, in the Anglican tradition, the Second Book of Homilies and the Articles of Religion make it quite clear how important discipline is for the health of the body. This discipline has to do with access to the Sacraments, and with people who are called to ministry of one kind or another. It has to do with family life, and with people called to singleness or to marriage. And no church can effectively be church without this kind of discipline. Of course this discipline is to be soundly and biblically based, but it also has to be exercised. In the Anglican Communion there has been an attempt to develop the so-called 'instruments of communion', whether that is the Lambeth Conference, or the meeting of Primates, or the role of the Archbishop of Canterbury. All of these have been designed so that there may be proper discipline in the church. But these instruments cannot work unless we give heed to the apostolic testimony, unless the Bible is central to discipline as to everything else in the Christian life and in the church. If the apostolic testimony is not central, these instruments just become formal, they become mere processes. We have seen attempts recently to turn them simply into processes but discipline is not just about process; it is about the faith by which the church continues to live.

8.   Strengths and weaknesses of Anglicanism

In all of this, the church is a missionary body: it does not just exist for itself; it exists for the world round about. Here there are some strengths in Anglicanism, but also some weaknesses. The strengths are the ability to relate to community, to work with the grain, to be able to access people at times that are very important for them, whether these are rites of passage, times of bereavement, or civic watersheds. These things are great advantages, and we have taken good care to see that we use them.

But if this is strength, there is also a weakness, and I think this weakness has been revealed in the situation that we face. The tendency to Erastianism in Anglicanism (to be too closely related to the State) has led, in certain contexts, to the tendency to capitulate to culture. I do not believe that this has to do with this or that issue, with this person or that church. It is actually endemic. It is a tendency, a fault line, that will keep appearing.[5]

8.1.   A prophetic calling

In this context what do Christians have to say to their own culture? This is where we have to be prophetic within our own church, and to our own ecclesiastical tradition. We can learn from other Christians how to be prophetic, and how to work against the grain as well as with it. Consider the sort of legislation that is being passed in Parliament, about the beginning or the end of life, or the public doctrine of marriage, for example. Christians will find that they cannot continue to work with the grain. We will have to say, 'Enough is enough. We now need to bear prophetic witness in this

---

[5] Ephraim Radner and Philip Turner, *The Fate of Communion: The Agony of Anglicanism and the Future of a Global Church* (Grand Rapids: Eerdmans, 2006)

matter to the culture around us, to the state, even within the church.' In this, of course, we can learn from Christians who are persecuted for their faith, and we have a great cloud of witnesses in that respect. The more I consider the kind of cultural confrontation that is coming up, the less likely it seems to me that the current state of affairs can continue. I shall be very sorry if and when it ends, but we have to think about the challenges that are coming up.

8.2. The uniqueness of Christ

One of the great challenges for the future, in addition to the ones that I have just mentioned, is the whole question of the uniqueness of Christ. In my Chavasse Lectures at Wycliffe Hall, I took that as my subject, because I believe that maintaining the uniqueness of Christ in Britain will become nearly as hard as it was in the Roman Empire[6]. Every attempt we make to relate to the civic authorities, everything we say in Parliament, whatever we read or write in the newspapers will be subject to this question. Our chaplaincy arrangements are in jeopardy. Wherever we find that we are working in a situation of partnership with the state, or receiving funding from some public body, we will find that the apostolic testimony about the uniqueness of Christ is in danger. And we will then have to decide whether to continue to work with the grain and to compromise, or to take a clear stand. That will be a call on our resources. We will lose many of the advantages that we already have. People will accuse us of things like being sectarian, which is, of course, the worst thing for an Anglican! But whether those accusations are truthful or not is not so important as it sometimes seems.

---

[6] The 2007 Chavasse Lectures at Wycliffe Hall, Oxford are to be published as *The Unique and Universal Christ: Jesus in a Plural World* (Milton Keynes: Paternoster, 2008)

9.   Conclusion

In conclusion, unity is very precious for us as believers. We
cherish it. But we do not cherish it above truth. There are certain
things that can disrupt fellowship. In the New Testament two
things are consistently presented as being able to disrupt
fellowship. One is persistent and systematic false teaching
whatever the scope of it might be. And the other is persistent
sexual immorality. Of course, there is always repentance and
forgiveness, as 1 John tells us. Exclusion from the church, or from
what the church does, from the Sacraments, from the Christian
life, need not be permanent. Indeed, we can say that any such
disruption must be for the sake of, and in the hope of, restoration.
But those are the two things that do disrupt fellowship, and we
must take this very seriously in our present situation.

LATIMER STUDIES